HOLLY-JANE RAHLENS

ONE FINE DAY

Or How I Learned to Walk Straight

Illustrations: Lene Hahne
Map p. 4: Per Illum

TR
TEEN READERS

Holly-Jane Rahlens:
One Fine Day
Teen Readers, Level 4

Editorial consultants:

Margaret Kersten, KLETT
Catherine Candea, BORDAS
Annemarie Zinck, ASCHEHOUG A/S
Ulla Malmmose, ASCHEHOUG A/S

Cover photo, © Ekkehard König
Photo, page 58 © United Press International Photo
Photo, page 58 © Nordisk Pressefoto A/S
Photo, page 59 © Nordisk Pressefoto A/S
Photo, page 60 © Nordisk Pressefoto A/S
Photo, page 61 © 1964, J.H.S. 198, Queens, New York
Photo, page 61 © SFB/Pressebild Kindermann

ISBN Denmark 87-11-08164-3
www.easyreader.dk

Printed in Denmark by
Sangill Grafisk Produktion, Holme-Olstrup

Autor/Literatur/Quellen

Prof. Dr. Uwe Böschemeyer, geboren 1939, studierte evangelische Theologie und widmete sich Studien in Philosophie und Psychologie. 1975 erwarb er bei Prof. Viktor E. Frankl in Wien sein Zertifikat in Logotherapie und Existenzanalyse und wurde von ihm 1980 auch zur Lehre der existenzanalytischen Logotherapie autorisiert. 1982 gründete er das *Hamburger Institut für Existenzanalyse und Logotherapie*, 2006 die *Akademie für Wertorientierte Persönlichkeitsbildung* in Lüneburg. 2000 erhielt er das *Europäische Zertifikat für Psychotherapie* (ECP), wurde 2006 zum Rektor der *Europäischen Akademie für Wertorientierte Persönlichkeitsbildung* in Salzburg ernannt und 2007 in die österreichische Psychotherapeutenliste aufgenommen. Schwerpunkte seiner Arbeit sind die von ihm entwickelten Konzepte *Wertimagination* und *Wertorientierte Persönlichkeitsbildung*. Seit 1975 ist er wissenschaftlicher Mitarbeiter des Hamburger Abendblatts, bekannt durch Radiointerviews sowie zahlreiche Bücher und Aufsätze.

Vom Typ zum Original. Die neun Gesichter der Seele und das eigene Gesicht, BoD
Neu beginnen! Konkrete Hilfen in Wende- und Krisenzeiten, Lahr 1996
Das Leben meint mich. Meditationen für den neuen Tag, Hamburg 2004
Das Leben meint uns. 111 Ermutigungen für Paare, München 2003
Sich selbst bejahen, Hamburg 2002
Die Sprache der Träume, Hamburg 2002
Sinn für mein Leben finden, Hamburg 2002
Die Kraft deiner Gedanken, Hamburg 2002
U. B./M. Van Cappellen: Bei sich beginnen. 17 Wege zum Glück, Hamburg 2004
Unsere Tiefe ist hell. Wertimagination – ein Schlüssel zur inneren Welt, München 2005
Worauf es ankommt. Werte als Wegweiser, München 2006
Gottesleuchten. Begegnungen mit dem unbewussten Gott in unserer Seele, München 2007
Sag Ja und lebe! Meditationen für jeden Tag, Hamburg 2007
Gespräche der inneren Welt, BoD, Hamburg 2008
Vertrau der Liebe, die dich trägt, München 2009

1 *U. Böschemeyer,* Vom Typ zum Original. Die neun Gesichter der Seele und das eigene Gesicht, BoD.
2 *C. G. Jung,* Heros und Mutterarchetyp, Grundwerk, Band 8, S. 13.
3 Eine Reihe der „goldenen Worte" habe ich dem anregenden Buch „Das Enneagramm der Weisheit – Spirituelle Schätze aus drei Jahrtausenden" (hrsg. von *Marion Küstenmacher*), München 1996, entnommen.
4 *E. C. Hirsch,* Der Witzableiter oder Schule des Gelächters, Hamburg 1985, 2. Aufl., S. 263.

Bildnachweis/Impressum/ Informationen

Bildnachweis
Toma Babovic, Bremen: Titel untere Reihe Mitte und S. 83; Gisela Caspersen, Hamburg: Titel mittlere Reihe li. und S. 45, Titel mittlere Reihe re. und S. 63; Andreas Riedmiller, Oberzollhaus: Titel obere Reihe li. und S. 17, Titel obere Reihe re. und S. 37, Titel mittlere Reihe Mitte und S. 55, Titel untere Reihe re. und S. 91; Otto Stadler, Geisenhausen: Titel obere Reihe Mitte und S. 29, Titel untere Reihe li. und S. 73

Bibliographische Information der Deutschen Bibliothek
Die Deutsche Bibliothek verzeichnet diese Publikation in der Deutschen Nationalbibliographie; detaillierte bibliographische Daten sind im Internet über http://dnb.ddb.de abrufbar.

ISBN 978-3-8319-0090-9

2. Auflage 2009

Gestaltung: Büro Brückner + Partner, Bremen
Satz: KCS GmbH, Buchholz/Hamburg
Lithographie: ORC, Offset-Repro im Centrum, Hamburg
Druck: Tutte Druckerei GmbH, Salzweg bei Passau
Bindung: Buchbinderei S. R. Büge GmbH, Celle

Weiterführende Informationen über Theorie und Praxis der Wertimagination erhalten Sie hier:
Hamburger Institut für Existenzanalyse und Logotherapie
Akademie für Wertorientierte Persönlichkeitsbildung
Barckhausenstraße 20
21335 Lüneburg
Telefon: 04131/403844
Telefax: 04131/403845
E-Mail: sekretariat@boeschemeyer.de
www.logotherapie-hamburg.de
www.wertorientierte-persoenlichkeitsbildung.de

11.05.2012

Die Frage: WAS ist mit MEINEM ICH?

Ich wollte geliebt werden (von D.S.!) und werde jetzt (von Hans) geliebt. Reicht das nicht?

Ich wollte mich mit DS. unterhalten kommunizieren?

kann ich nicht mit Hans kommunizieren?

Ich wollte Zärtlichkeit und Stärke ▷

und Hans? ↑

Beobachter / Analytiker

Gefühl?

Was will ICH?

Ich habe gemerkt, dass ich mich an-deren anpasse[(n) will!] und mich verändern möchte. Wie Wachs in den Händen oder Ton!

ABER!

WAS ist MEIN Weg? ← Vernunft!

ABER!

Im Moment "spüre" / denke / fühle ich, dass - egal, womit ich mich bisher beschäftigt habe, an einem

Bild (Puzzle) passt, fügt!
Auch wie ich mich entscheide und wofür
und warum!
z.B. das mit Hans (kurz vor Borkum)

ABOUT THE AUTHOR

HOLLY-JANE RAHLENS grew up in New York City. After graduating college she moved to Berlin, Germany, where she works as a writer and producer/director for radio and television. She has also appeared as an actress in various theater, film and television productions. Her one-woman show of 'ONE FINE DAY, or How I Learned to Walk Straight' premiered in Berlin in 1989. It has since been adapted for German television.

The *Teen Reader* edition of *One Fine Day, or How I Learned to Walk Straight* has been adapted by the author from her one-woman stage comedy. Vocabulary and sentence structure have been simplified to provide easy reading for students of English.

This reader is accompanied by a tape cassette containing the entire text, narrated by the author herself, and including authentic music from the 1960s.

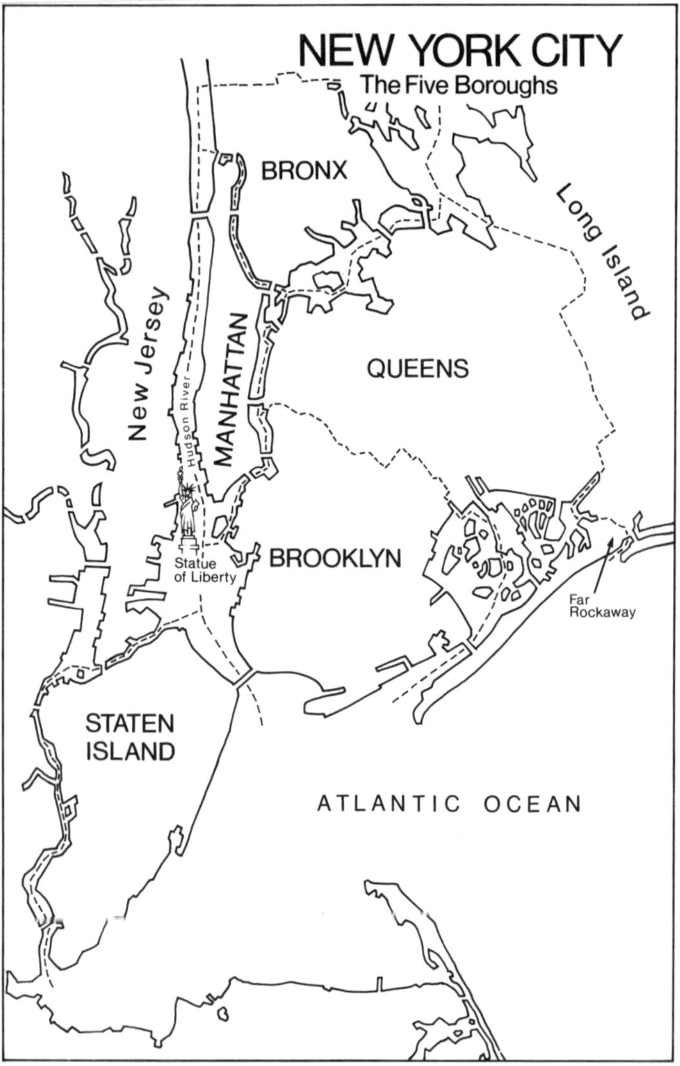
NEW YORK CITY
The Five Boroughs
BRONX
Long Island
New Jersey
Hudson River
MANHATTAN
QUEENS
Statue of Liberty
BROOKLYN
Far Rockaway
STATEN ISLAND
ATLANTIC OCEAN

1. The Narrator

A friend of mine, this computer expert, who thinks I'm the most intelligent woman he ever met, recently asked me what my *IQ* was. So I told him of course. I said, "It's 148." My high intelligence quotient must certainly have left a deep impression on his somewhat lower 123 IQ mind, because whenever I do or say anything stupid, which unfortunately happens a lot these days, he *nudges* me in the ribs and says with a laugh, "For a 148er that was truly out of character."

Believe me, it's quite a hard job living up to the reputation of *the brainy*. Of course if I really had an IQ of 148 it would be far easier to keep up my image, but to tell the truth, I don't even know what my IQ is. Although we sweated through dozens of intelligence tests in the late Fifties and early Sixties, the results were kept under lock and key.

One day, however, when I was thirteen years old and in the 8th grade, I remember *sneaking* up to my teacher's desk while she was watering the plants in the back of the room. Pretending to sharpen my pencil in the waste basket, I examined a list of numbers in a book she had left open on her desk. I was certain the numbers were our IQ scores and therefore the secret to our future lives. Next to my name I saw the number 1-3-2. Well,

---

IQ, Intelligence Quotient, a number that measures a person's intelligence. The average is 110.
nudge, push lightly with elbow
the brainy, very intelligent people
sneak, to walk very quietly so no one hears or sees you when doing something you shouldn't be doing

maybe it was 1-2-3 – even at that early age I was quite short-sighted. And maybe it wasn't even our IQ scores. It could have been just about anything. In any case, I bent down to get a better look, when suddenly Miss Cohen, my teacher, called out, "What are you doing at my desk, young lady?"

"Oh nothing, Miss Cohen," I answered instantly. "I was just sharpening my pencil and some of the *shavings* fell on your desk and I was wiping it off so you wouldn't get dirty."

She smiled and thanked me for my consideration. And I went back to my seat having then and there decided for no reason whatsoever that my IQ was going to be at least 123, maybe 132, and even 148 if I was in the mood.

In any case, I felt very smart, but not so much due to my new intelligence quotient, but rather because I had once again proven how easy it is to be a *cunning fibber.* In short: I tell lies. They come in all sizes and shapes. For example, not only did I lie to my teacher, but I've lied to you too. Take a look at the very first sentence of this story. That computer friend of mine who asked me what my IQ was, well, he does not consider me the most intelligent woman he ever met. I'm only the second-most. The most intelligent woman is a politi-

---

cunning, smart in a clever way
fibber, a person who tells little lies

shavings

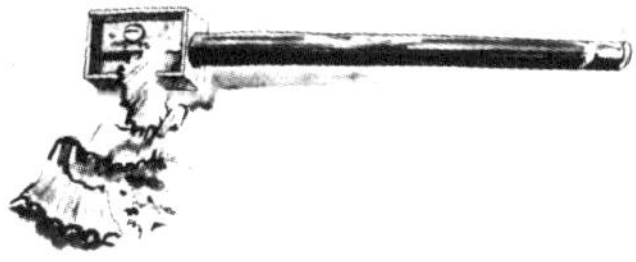

cian he once met on a TV talk show where they were both guests. But you see, it doesn't really matter. If he hadn't met her, if he hadn't been invited to that talk show, I would be the most intelligent woman he ever met. So this is why I can say with a *clear conscience* that I am.

Okay, you're probably wondering why on earth I'm telling you this. You see, I've been asked to tell you a story about something that really happened to me over twenty-five years ago when I was thirteen years old. And since deep down somewhere I am an honest *gal* I thought it best to let you know before I even begin the tale that I'm not going to tell you the truth.

As you may have realized, I have always had a hard time telling the difference between what is and what could be, between what really happened and what might have happened. And to be honest, I don't think it matters at all. But even if I can't give you an exact account of the story, I promise to try my best to let you understand what those events felt like to me. And if you ask me, (or any good *psychologist*) that's what really counts, right?

And I do remember what it felt like. I once read somewhere that it's very healthy practice for adults to stay in touch with their younger selves, and I'm glad to say that I'm still good friends with the thirteen-year-old I once was. Sometimes, I must admit, she gets on my nerves. Like in the early hours of the morning

---

clear conscience, without feeling guilt
gal, (slang) girl
psychologist, a person who can help you understand your feelings and thoughts better

when she wakes me up with her nightmares. But then other times she's a real sweetheart. The other day, for instance, while I was in this store shopping for a fancy dress, she happened to come by to say hello. I had a big date that evening with this fellow and I wanted to wear something special. So for hours I'd been trying on *slinky*, silky, black dresses, but they either left too little room around the hips or too much on top. And, believe me, it was very frustrating, because I wanted to look great but I felt so out of shape.

And then suddenly she was there, my thirteen-year-old self, looking at me in the dressing-room mirror. She smiled, stood up on tiptoe and whispered in my ear, "Come on already, lighten up! All you have to do is remember what it was like to be in love for the first time and everything'll be okay. Forget the dress. He'll like you anyway."

The beauty of "first love," you see, was her very own specialty and it was very sweet of her to remind me of it. So I decided against a fancy dress and bought a new computer text program instead (which, as luck would have it, turned out to have a *virus* or something). In any case, later that evening, wearing my simple black cotton *jump suit*, I did, in fact, remember what it was like to be in love again for the first time.

I and my thirteen-year-old self have recently begun to compare notes and I've realized that we have much more in common than just a flat chest. And I like the

---

slinky, gracefully tight-fitting
virus, a very, very small living organism that can cause sickness in people, but may also be used to describe something that makes computers go crazy
jump suit, one-piece garment for the whole body

little dear, much more so, for instance, than my seventeen-year-old self who was a rather boring, *irritable* kid, always studying for *trigonometry* tests, biting her nails, forgetting to brush her teeth and walking around with *runs in her stockings*. But even she was better than my twenty-five-year-old self who until today remains a real threat to me. Now she was a pain in the neck, a jealous and dependent young lady pretending she wasn't.

And then, of course, there's my present self. She thinks she's the center of the universe. She is also thoughtless of others, vain, self-centered, mean, and in all respect to her better qualities, much too hard on herself. She's the one who spends her time trying on dresses that won't fit and spends her money on computer programs that have the *sniffles*. She's the one who pays her bills on time and tries to do a *workout* every morning, but she has never learned to drive a car or to eat with *chopsticks*.

I'm telling you this because this present self is going to describe to you what it felt like to be thirteen years old over twenty-five years ago and I thought it would be nice for you to know a little something about your narrator. She would like so very, very much to tell you

---

irritable, quick to anger
trigonometry, the branch of mathematics which deals with the relations between the sides and the angles of triangles
runs in stockings, a long rip or tear in a stocking
sniffles, a running nose; a cold
workout, physical exercizes to keep your body healthy and fit
chopsticks, pair of thin sticks held in one hand, used by Chinese people to lift food to the mouth

the truth, the whole truth and nothing but, yet already she's changing reality, rearranging her *memory*. For example, she has just decided to begin her tale with the words "one fine day." That's terrible! She's hopeless! She knows perfectly well that when the story began it was really cold, cloudy and *drizzly*!

---

memory, what you remember and keep in your head
drizzly, rain softly

2. One Fine Day Walking to the Park

One fine day back in the early Sixties, all the way back in New York City, I and my best friend Judy O'Reilly are walking down our red and gold tree-lined street. It's a brilliant and crisp autumn afternoon - royal blue sky, *puffy*, white clouds, bright, stark sunlight. The street's in Far Rockaway. If you look at a map of New York you'll see that Far Rockaway is situated on the most southeastern tip of the *borough* of Queens, right on the Atlantic coast and at the most important border in the whole world - the one that separates New York City from Long Island and therefore from the rest of the universe.

The beach is a fifteen-minute walk from our street which runs along the *elevated subway*. At our corner, standing in front of The Sugar Bowl, our neighborhood candy store, if you try very hard and if a train isn't passing by at that very moment, you might possibly hear monster birds screaming at killer sharks, or *tidal waves* rolling in from Europe crashing on the cliffs. And when you take in a deep breath you can almost smell the ocean, the *seaweed*, the popcorn and cotton candy sold on the *boardwalk*, and - iieehh - a dead *jellyfish* washed up on shore.

---

puffy, big and full
borough, New York City is divided into five boroughs or parts: Manhattan, Brooklyn, Queens, Staten Island and the Bronx.
elevated subway, see picture, page 16
tidal wave, extremely rare, large ocean wave usually caused by an earthquake
seaweed, a plant that grows at the sea
boardwalk, *jellyfish*, see picture, page 14

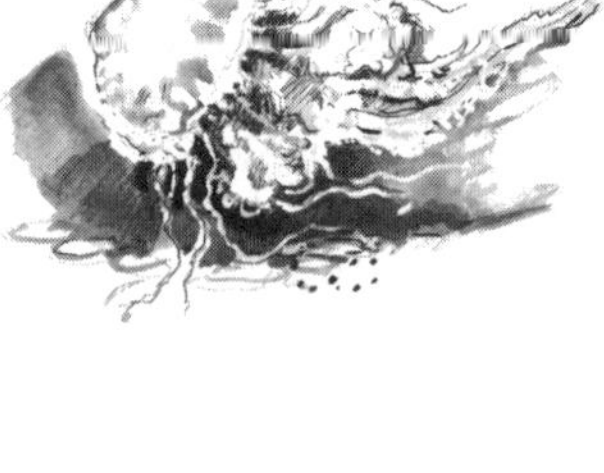

jellyfish

But Judy and I are not going to the beach. We've decided to spend our Sunday afternoon in the park up the block. Judy, a roundish girl with long, shiny red hair, green eyes, a mouth full of silver *braces* and a heart of gold, is eating an *ice-cream cone*. I'm wearing my thick, curly, dark hair pulled back in a *pony-tail* because I don't know what else to do with it. I used to be an attractive kid, but now I'm growing too fast around the hips and too slow on top, pimples line my forehead and my nose is getting a bit too big for my liking.

"It's in the family," says Grandma with her Yiddish-Russian accent. "It's a beautiful nose, magnificent."

I wish I could believe her.

"*Oy vay iz mir*! What's wrong with having a nose a person can find, I ask you?! Look, *bubeleh*, you don't like it, you want a new one? Ask your cheap father to go and buy you a new one when you're sweet sixteen."

But now, walking next to Judy, I'm not thinking of noses. I'm trying very hard to blow huge pink bubbles with my chewing-gum. And I'm carrying my transistor radio, and yes, I can hear The Chiffons singing "One Fine Day."

So there we are, dancing to the music, Judy in her white *sneakers* and me in my – oh goodness, what are those terrible things attached to my feet? I'm wearing

---

braces, here: wires used for straightening teeth
ice cream cone, *pony-tail*, see picture, page 16
oy vay iz mir, Yiddish expression of dismay
bubeleh, Yiddish for darling
sneakers, see picture, page 16

elevated subway
ponytail
ice-cream cone
sneakers
ONE WAY
THE SUGAR BOWL
CANDY STORE
PEPSI
DENTI
SALON

the ugliest, most disgusting, heaviest pair of *orthopedic shoes* a tender-hearted thirteen-year-old can imagine! No one can fail to see that I'm *pigeon-toed*.

Pigeon-toed! Uugghh! It's a word that even today makes me fall into a state of despair. Well, perhaps I'm *exaggerating*. Being pigeon-toed is certainly not the worst thing that can happen to a child. But still, how would you like some doctor to twist your feet all the time with his icy cold fingers? Or force you to pick up a ping-pong ball with your toes for fifteen minutes every day, although all you really want to do is stretch out on your bed and read the newest 'Intimate Confession' love comic? Or have all the kids on the block laugh at you when you run? Or wear orthopedic shoes to the Thanksgiving Day dance when all the other girls will be wearing fancy pumps and high-heels?

But now, walking down the street with Judy on the way to the park on this brilliant autumn afternoon, I have other things on my mind. I'm in love. For the very first time. Okay, two weeks ago my biology teacher, Mr. Martin, was the man of my dreams, but that doesn't count. Now I'm really in love, in love with Mark Lieberman, tall, blue-eyed, sure-footed,

---

orthopedic shoes, shoes worn to correct a walking problem
pigeon-toed, walk with your toes turned in like a *pigeon*
exaggerate, to make something bigger or more important than it is

pigeon

charming Mark Lieberman, the captain of the school's basketball team.

"You think Mark will be in the park? Yes or no?" I hear my little self say to my companion. Judy, an earnest, down-to-earth type of few words, pauses before she answers.

"I *dunno*," she finally replies.

"Oh, but he usually is on the weekend!"

"So then he'll be there!"

And then after a moment's pause she adds, "But it's kind of cool outside."

"Oh, but they even play outside when it's ten degrees below zero. Don't you think he has the most *stunning* nose? Oh, God, Judy, did I tell you he said hello to me in the cafeteria on Friday and I almost spilled my pea soup?"

"You told me at least a hundred times, Mother of God! But actually you're right. His nose really is nice."

---

dunno, in good language: don't know
stunning, very attractive

3. Me, Mark and the Fence

Mark is in the park that brilliant autumn day, playing basketball with the boys. Judy and I walk over to the fence and join our girlfriends watching the game. Everyone is there: Ellen, Carol, Lisa, the twins Sandy and Sue Silver, and Patsy, too, wearing her hair in a *beehive* with a *bow* on top.

Suddenly, the basketball bangs on the fence and we all jump back and scream. Mark looks towards us, sees me and waves.

"Well at least he knows who you are. Maybe you do have a chance," says Judy. And my heart skips a beat. But that's nothing compared to what happens during the break. Mark could come over to any of the girls standing at the fence, but what does he do? He comes to me, to me! To little old pigeon-toed me.

"Hi. Do you have any more bubble gum?" he asks politely.

"Sure, here," I say, pulling a piece out of the pocket of my shocking red pants. And what does he do? He grabs my hand, drags me a few feet away and starts *dribbling* the basketball with me! I mean, the only boy

---

dribble, bounce a basketball

that ever wanted to dribble with me was my older brother Davey, and that's because no one else was around.

I manage to dribble the ball away from him, but then he grabs me from behind and the ball drops and rolls away. But instead of going after it, Mark tightens his grip and leans me back against him. And there we stand and stand and stand. Me, Mark and the fence.

This was not the first time a boy had ever touched me. The past year I'd been invited to many a party, had been in many a dark basement playroom dancing arm-in-arm with someone or other. But, aahh, this was *seventh heaven* – Mark leaning against the fence, my back leaning against him, his arms around me. This was the first time anyone had ever really touched me like that. And no one has ever touched me quite that way since.

"HEY, EVERYBODY!! GET A LOOK AT THE FEET OVER THERE!"

I'm brought back down to earth by the barking voice of Fat-Face-Frankie Moronelli, the *crude* and hopelessly overweight school terrorizer.

"Everybody, look at those feet," he shouts out, pointing to my orthopedic shoes. And pointing to me he says, "Hey you! Yeah you! I'm talkin' to you, pigeon-toed. Pigeon-toed. Pigeon-toed."

The other boys join in, repeating the word "pigeon-toed" over and over again. My face turns red and my eyes fill with tears of shame. Why are they hurting me like this? What did I ever do to Frankie to deserve this

---

seventh heaven, great happiness
crude, having no manners

treatment? And where's Mark? Why doesn't he save me? But his arms aren't around me anymore. He's standing a few feet away, watching silently from the sidelines. Well, I'll have to defend myself.

"Oh shut up, Fatso," I hear myself screaming in Fat-Face-Frankie Moronelli's *bloated* face. The word "Fatso" is to Frankie what "pigeon-toed" is to me.

"You talkin' to me? Who's Fatso?" he says with a threatening voice, clapping the sweaty palms of his hands to my chest.

"You think you're so smart, pigeon-toed? Huh? So come on, let's do 'it.' You *wanna* do 'it'? It'll only take two minutes. Just two minutes!"

I am completely and utterly shocked. Do "it"? In two minutes? I give Fat-Face-Frankie a push that sends him spinning, and Judy and I *dash* away for dear life.

---

bloated, fat
wanna, in good language: want to
dash, run very swiftly on light feet

4. Up on the Roof

Judy and I hide away from Fat-Face-Frankie Moronelli at our favorite spot looking over Far Rockaway from my apartment house roof.

"Isn't Frankie just disgusting?" I say, lighting up a cigarette I stole from my mother. My eyes grow dark and earnest.

"Judy, how long do you really think it takes to do 'it'?"

"Gee, how should I know?" she answers. But then she thinks hard and adds, "But I think it takes my parents a little longer."

"Yeah? How much longer?"

"I dunno 'cause they always have a Frank Sinatra record on and I can't hear."

I sigh, smoke the cigarette I shouldn't be smoking, crack some bubbles with a new piece of gum, turn on the transistor radio, and worrying about "it" I listen to the Shirelles singing "Will You (Still) Love Me Tomorrow?"

"No!" I suddenly cry out with the authority of a scientist who has just made an earthshaking discovery. "No, no, no! It most definitely takes longer! Look, Judy, these songs in the radio are proof. I can't believe that all these songs would be written and sung about something that only takes two minutes. It just doesn't make sense!"

"Listen," Judy interrupts, "if you're into worrying, worry about like why Mark didn't defend you before or anything."

"Oh come on, Judy. Why should he get in trouble

with Fat-Face-Frankie too?"

"Because I don't like him, that's why! Look, Patsy told me in the park that he's been going with Glenda Lapidus for at least two weeks. She even has his *ID bracelet*. As your best friend I thought I should tell you. I'm real sorry."

"GLENDA LAPIDUS!?! That *snob*!?!" Oh, how could I ever compete with Glenda Lapidus, who's not only rich and an exotic *southern belle* from *Tallahassee*, but a cheerleader too. Everyone knew that the cheerleaders – those ra-ra-siss-boom-ba girls at all the sports events who supported the boys with their dances and shouts – were the prettiest, most graceful, most popular and most admired girls at the whole school. And one thing was sure: none of them was pigeon-toed.

"Forget him," Judy says.

"I won't. I can't. I'll fight for him!"

"Fight for him? Listen, what's your IQ anyway?"

"My IQ? Uuhh ... 123. No, I mean 148. Why?"

"Because for a 148er you're pretty stupid. That's why!"

---

snob, a person who doesn't like people he or she thinks are lower on the social scale
southern belle, a pretty girl or woman from America's South
Tallahassee, the capital of Florida

ID bracelet

5. A Typical Sunday at Home

Disturbed by Mark's interest in Glenda, I spend the rest of the afternoon *sulking* at home. My brother Davey, a shy and withdrawn boy, is away learning to become a *forward* and *outgoing* man on a weekend camping trip. My sister Joycey, just a year and a half younger than me but ten times sweeter, begs me to help her with her math homework. She's weak in arithmetic and will never pass her test if I don't help, but still I refuse.

And there's Mom, as usual cleaning the apartment. Carefully she dusts the bookcase, taking out each and every *Harold Robbins* and *James Michener*. She just turned forty-two so her hair is probably gray, but you can't tell because she dyes it cherry-blonde. Well, she's a working woman, a secretary, and she has to look good! Oh, dear Mom, wasting her Sundays with dusting, washing, sweeping, ironing, cooking lamb chops. She tries her best and gets so little in return.

Uuh ooh, there's Dad, lying all over the couch. His bathrobe is half-open so if you look the wrong way you can see his white boxer shorts underneath. He's smoking a smelly cigar, watching a football game on TV, reading the sports scores in 'The New York Times' all at the same time, plus he's *yelling* at my mother to stop dusting the TV for God's sake while he's watching!

---

sulk, be silent and unfriendly because of bad mood
forward, eager
outgoing, friendly
Harold Robbins/James Michener, American bestseller writers
yell, scream, shout

Dad's a *gifted* salesman. He can sell anything from ladies' winter coats and sewing-machines to *encyclopedias* and life insurance – that is, if he has a job. When he does, he's generous and funny. But when he doesn't, uuh ooh, just watch that blood pressure rise. Right now he's forty-five and out of work – in other words, he's in a bad, bad mood.

The cooking timer in the kitchen rings and my mother yells, "Supper's ready. Come on girls, set the table!"

"What are you sulking about?" my father asks me over dinner.

"She wouldn't help me with math," Joycey says.

My mother looks at me with concern. "Princess, is there something wrong?"

"Oh Mommy," I cry out, "Oh Mommy, can't I get high-heels? All the girls are *gonna* be wearing them to the Thanksgiving Day dance."

"How many times do we have to say no!" shouts my father.

"Jerry," my mother shouts back at my father, "don't scream at her!"

"You're killing my ears!" shouts Joycey.

"Sweetheart," says my mother to me in a softer tone, "Dr. Friedman said you can't wear high-heels until your *arches* strengthen. You know that."

"He also said she'd grow out of it," my father *snaps* at

---

gifted, having a natural ability for something
encyclopedia, a book of information arranged alphabetically
gonna, in good language: going to
arch, here: the curve in the inner side of the foot
snap, here: speak suddenly in a violent way

me. "What's taking so long? What does it take to walk straight? Why can't my daughter walk straight? Do you know how much money we're *dishing out* to that doctor?"

"Oh how could you be so cruel?" my mother cries out. "It's not her fault. If you finally got a decent job maybe we could move into an apartment where the trains don't always come crashing through the bedroom window, and maybe we could finally buy her a new pair of orthopedic shoes."

"I DON'T WANT ORTHOPEDIC SHOES!" I yell at the top of my lungs, "I want high-heels! High-heels!"

Peppy, our crazy salt-and-pepper schnauzer, barks hysterically. Joycey *chokes* on a lamb chop and I run into the bathroom, lock myself in tight and cry my eyes out!

---

dish out, (slang) spend a lot of money
choke, what happens when something gets caught in the throat

6. How to Become a Cheerleader by Really Trying

The next day at school, thank goodness, things take a turn for the better. In gym class I manage to dribble the basketball away from my enemy Glenda Lapidus and score the winning point for my team. Her face turns green! On top of that - and now, finally, I'm coming to the heart of my tale - our gym teacher, Mrs. Woo-Chang, tells us that there will be try-outs for the cheerleaders because one of the girls has switched schools. A new cheerleader? Oh, my God, if only . . .

"I think I'm gonna try out for the cheerleaders," I explain to Judy in the girl's *locker* room. "That way I can see Mark all the time and have more of a chance of winning him back."

"First of all, you can't win him back because you never had him in the first place," Judy says while slipping into her dress. "Second, be sensible. You have the spirit to be a cheerleader but not the feet. They'd all laugh at you. And third, could you please do my buttons in the back?"

At that very moment, awful Glenda Lapidus appears, all polished and perfect, her *page-boy haircut* shiny and in place.

locker

page-boy haircut

"Just in case you're thinking of trying out," she says, "don't. We won't accept any pigeon-toes on the cheerleading team." Then turning to Judy she *drawls*, "And you'd have to lose at least five hundred pounds before we took you!" And she's gone.

I have never seen Judy so mad. "Five hundred pounds! Just who the hell does she think she is anyway?" she says so everyone can hear. And then right then and there my life changes utterly and completely.

"Go for it," Judy cries out. "Go, go, go for it! We're gonna make a cheerleader out of you, pigeon-toed or not. We'll show them!"

My days are now spent learning, memorizing and practicing the complicated jumps, steps and hand movements. Whether I'm up on the roof with Judy, down in the subway with my mother, babysitting, visiting Dr. Friedman, walking Peppy, or in my room – everywhere I am, I practice the cheers. It goes without saying that I make everyone around me crazy, especially when I suddenly burst out with a cheer. For example,

"When you're up, you're up,
When you're down, you're down,
But no sweat, boys, you're the best in town!
Yeah, team!"

Or:
"Give me a T
T.

---

drawl, speak in a long and drawn-out way as people often do in the American South

Give me an O
O.
Give me a P
P.
Give me an S
S.
What's that spell?
Tops!
What's that spell?
TOPS!
Come on, boys, you're the *cream of the crop*!
Yeah, team!!"

Indeed, life is quite *exhausting*. In fact, it's so exhausting, I more or less forget about Mark – that is, until the morning of the try-outs. To Glenda's horror, Mark wishes me good luck on the school bus. But then to my horror, Fat-Face-Frankie Moronelli pushes me off the bus, and I hurt my knee.

"Pretend it never happened," Judy advises me.

"But it hurts like hell," I cry out in despair.

"Mind over matter," is her wise reply. "I mean, do you want to be a cheerleader or not?"

"Of course I do."

"Then fight for your right to the last!"

I have a lot of competition that afternoon – there are fifteen other girls all fighting to the last for their right to be a cheerleader too. I'm a bit nervous and my knee

---

cream of the crop, the very best
exhausting, very tiring

hurts, but Judy's out there *rooting* for me so things could be worse.

The jury is made up of Mrs. Lu Woo-Chang, my gym teacher, Miss Betty Donohue, the coach of the cheerleading team, and Mr. Wilfredo Rodriguez, the basketball coach. First they have all of us do the cheers together, then they separate us into smaller groups, and lastly, each of us goes out on the floor alone. I give it my best, what more can I say?

"You were fine, just fine," Judy congratulates. "They'd be crazy not to take you." And she's right, they would be crazy, and lucky for me they're not. I'm chosen as the new cheerleader!

"You'll have to improve your footwork," Mrs. Woo-Chang says, "but your enthusiasm and your energy make up for it more than enough. Good work. Good work."

"Good work, my foot! And who cares anyway about enthusiasm and energy?" Judy says later that day. "That's just half the battle. Now look, the first game of the season is next week. We have to sew your uniform, clear your forehead of those awful pimples and iron that curly hair of yours till it's straight. You have to be perfect and look perfect. Just think of Glenda and Fat-Face-Frankie out there. They want you to be a flop. We cannot give them that satisfaction, so..."

"Okay, okay," I break in, surprised by Judy's *verbosity*. "Alright already, where do we start?"

"With your toe exercises. Exercize fifteen minutes

---

root, here: encourage and support somebody
verbosity, using more words than needed

with the ping-pong ball every night before you go to sleep to give your toes added strength!"

I spend the next week preparing for my premiere, getting ready for the day I'll show Glenda and Fat-Face-Frankie, all of Benjamin Cardozo Junior High School, all of Far Rockaway, all of New York City, for all I care all of the entire *galaxy*, how gracefully and beautifully I can run and jump, how enthusiastically and energetically I can shout the cheers. In short, I'm gathering my strength for the first basketball game of the season, for the day on which Mark Lieberman, that prince of a boy, will fall in love with me forever and drop that snob Glenda like a hot potato. I have a goal in life.

---

galaxy, the system of stars and planets containing the Earth

7. The Most Important Day of My Life

The day of the season's first basketball game arrives, the truly most important day of my life until now. I wake up knowing that something absolutely unbelievable will happen to me and to me alone.

And it does.

In the hall on the way to math class I spot Mark. Butterflies begin *twittering* in my stomach, and I remember how one fine day, just a little over a week ago, he put his arms around me and pressed me close.

"I haven't seen you around lately," he says, shifting his feet back and forth.

"Oh, well, I've been real busy," I say.

"But I guess I'll see you later at the game," he says.

"Oh, sure, I'll be rooting for you." And then shifting my feet too, I add, "Nervous?"

"No, no, the team from Belle Harbor is a *cinch*."

"Oh," I say, lost in the deep blue of his eyes.

"Yeah, well."

"Yeah, well," I say, wondering if he wears long white boxer shorts like my father.

"You know," he says, "maybe we can go to The Sugar Bowl for an ice-cream soda after the game."

An ice-cream soda with Mark? My first real date ever! And with the captain of the basketball team. Oh, I just knew that this was going to be the most important day of my life. How will I ever be able to keep still until four p.m.?

---

twitter, move around in a very excited way
cinch, an easy job or a sure thing

C
C

School is complete torture. I cannot keep my attention on anything. All through History and English I look at my watch and dream of Mark holding me in his arms again. After lunch I have another three hours to go. Biology slowly comes to a close and somehow I manage to play my cello in Music Appreciation without Mr. Tagliofero noticing that I'm not working on the new Bach piece, but rather on the melody to "Be My Baby" from The Ronettes. The bell rings and there's just one more class to go – French, with *Mlle* Rabinowitz.

Mlle Rabinowitz *scolds* me for not paying attention in class. I try my best to repeat the verbs, but all I can really do is either see myself as the most perfect cheerleader on the basketball court or dream of Mark and my chocolate ice-cream soda with whipped cream and a très petite cherry on top.

"Je t'aime," I whisper to myself. "Je t'aime, Mark ... aahh, tu m'aimes aussi? Mais merci."

I look at my watch. There's just one half hour left before the game and I'm feverish with excitement. I'm just about to go to the girl's room for the tenth time that day when suddenly the loudspeaker switches on and we hear someone sobbing. Whoever could it be?

"Hey, you know what? I can't believe it! It's the *principal*. It's Mr. Dooling," Fat-Face-Frankie Moronelli exclaims with a wild grin.

The principal of our Junior High School crying?

Mlle = Mademoiselle, French for Miss
scold, tell someone he or she is doing something wrong and should stop doing it
principal, the head of a school

What could have happened? Soon enough he stops sobbing and with a solemn voice, deep and heavy, with a voice that makes our hair stand up straight, he says, "Children, I have an important announcement to make. The basketball game this afternoon has been *canceled*!"

I cannot believe my ears. My heart stops beating. "What?!" I cry out, "The basketball game is canceled?"

Everyone begins to whisper among themselves.

"Ssshhh," scolds Mlle Rabinowitz. "Silence, mes enfants. Silence! Oh keep still, for God's sake! Shut up!"

"The basketball game has been canceled," continues Mr. Dooling's voice over the loudspeaker. "Everything has been canceled. I'm sorry to say that the President of the United States of America, Mr. John F. Kennedy, has been shot in Dallas, Texas. We fear he's been *wounded fatally*. School buses will be waiting outside as usual. School is over for the day."

The loudspeaker dies out and the room is completely still. It's so still you can hear a feather drop.

"No!" I cry out, jumping up from my seat. "No, it can't be true! It's unfair! It's unfair! It's not true!"

"Please control yourself," Mlle Rabinowitz says to me. "Calm down. Everybody's unhappy about the President."

"The President?!?"

---

cancel, call off; make something not happen
wounded fatally, to be hurt so bad, it causes death; a very formal way of saying someone was killed

There I am, the prettiest little cheerleader you ever could see, with my short red skirt, my white sweatshirt with the big C across its middle, my perfect, straight, ironed-out pony-tail and my pimpleless face. And all I can think is, "Damn it. Damn it. Why did the President have to go and get himself shot today? Why not tomorrow?"

It was a black, black day indeed.

I'm standing in a Junior High School classroom in Far Rockaway, New York, somewhere on the most southeastern tip of the borough of Queens, listening to my French teacher sobbing and watching my classmates' tears fall on the French verbs in their notebooks.

And then I'm suddenly racing through the hall, looking for Mark. I find him standing tall and very serious with a whole group of kids, including Glenda. I boldly walk up to him.

"We can still go for an ice-cream soda, can't we?" I whisper in his ear ever so softly.

"How can you think of ice-cream at a time like this?" he answers with a shocked and far too loud voice. "We have to think about *John-John* and little *Caroline*. I'm gonna go and watch it on TV."

"Well I was too. We can watch it together at my house," I answer.

For a moment I see a "yes" light up in the deep blue of his eyes, but then Glenda, the silly *eavesdropper*, says,

---

John-John/Caroline, John F. Kennedy's children
eavesdropper, someone who listens secretly to other people's private conversations

"Oh, come to my house, Mark. We have color television."

It's not a big decision for Mark. How can he refuse an offer like color TV? Off he goes with Glenda, leaving poor, little me all alone.

I was never so hurt and disappointed in my entire life.

"I've been competing with a color TV. Would you believe it? I've been competing with a stupid color television," I say to Judy on the way home on the bus.

Outside, groups of adults are standing at every street corner. The shock of the President's death has brought them together.

"I will never forget this day as long as I live," I announce with great solemnity. "Friday, November 22, 1963."

"Forget him," Judy says. "Forget the *jerk*." She *pats* me on my back and gives me the biggest, silver-braced smile she can manage to give me on this most fateful and darkest of days.

---

jerk, (slang) idiot; someone very unacceptable
pat, touch lightly to express sympathy

8. How I Learned to Walk Straight

"Forget him," Judy has advised me. "Forget the jerk." And I do try to forget him. There is certainly enough going on in the world to help me. The following days my time is spent at school or in front of our black-and-white *portable television*. My brother Davey, my sister Joycey, Judy and I simply cannot stop watching the John F. Kennedy specials being *broadcasted* continuously. We were never before concerned with the elected chief of our country, but now we begin to put in our memories pictures of him as a baby, a school kid, a young college man, a handsome lieutenant saving the crew of his boat in the Pacific during World War II, a Congressman, a Senator, the President of the United States of America. On television we re-live in slow motion the *assassination*. "Look," we cry out, "that's where he waves to the people of Dallas. The first shot's gonna hit him any second now. Bang! Oh, watch his face twist with pain. He's gonna go down. There he goes. And now he falls back. Watch his head drop to *Jackie's* lap. Oh my God, look at all the blood on her brand-new hot pink *Coco Chanel* two-piece suit! It's disgusting! I can't look any more, tell me when it's over!!" We girls cover up our faces with our hands.

---

portable television, a television you can carry easily, usually small and cheap
broadcast, be shown on television
assassination, murder of a political or religious leader
Jackie, John F. Kennedy's wife
Coco Chanel, famous French fashion designer

"You can look now," Davey lets us know after a few seconds.

"Oh, it's Johnson," says Judy, "being sworn in as the new president.

"How boring," I add.

"He'll never be able to take Kennedy's place," exclaims my father. And he should know. I mean, Daddy wasn't voted Assistant Chairman of the local Democratic Club for nothing, was he?

"Oh what's this world coming to?" my mother says for the hundredth time since it all happened. She sighs, shakes her head and then lifts her *feather duster* up to the *venetian blinds* to wipe them clean, blind by blind.

All of us sit motionless in front of the TV. We watch the *funeral* and listen to the names of the foreign guests who have come to Arlington, Virginia, to say their last goodbyes. We see Lee Harvey Oswald, the Guilty One, the so-called Kennedy assassin. He's in *handcuffs* and there's a big crowd of policemen around him.

"Do you think he really killed him?" Joycey asks.

---

funeral, ceremony for burying a dead person
handcuffs, an instrument used to lock a prisoner's hands together

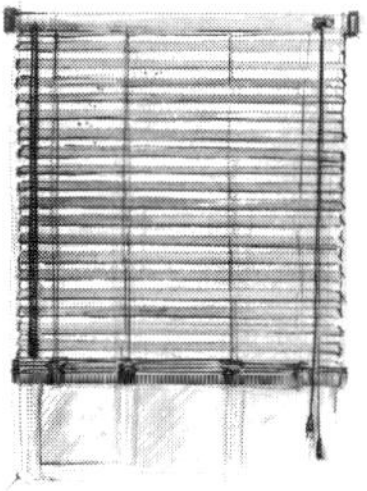
venetian blinds

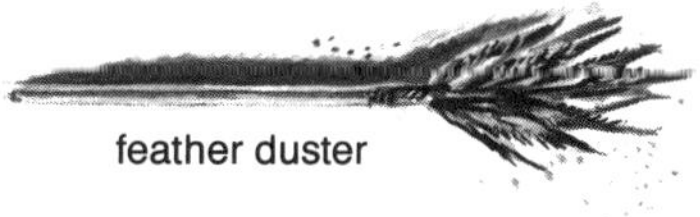
feather duster

"Of course, stupid," Davey answers. "Just look at those eyes."

"His eyes look pretty normal to me," I add.

"He's innocent until proven guilty," Judy remarks.

Suddenly the picture on the screen *jolts*. Was that a gun shot we heard? Dozens of men are running around on our black-and-white portable television while the camera tries its best to find a steady picture. It focuses and we see the Guilty One bent up in pain.

"Ooohhh!!" we all cry out together, finally understanding what we have just seen.

Oh my God! Davey, Joycey, Judy and I have just witnessed – live on TV – someone shooting Oswald.

A short while later a brand-new name enters our vocabulary forever: Jack Ruby, the Dallas nightclub owner who shot the President's assassin dead!

Indeed, all of this should make me forget Mark, but it doesn't quite do the job.

"You know, maybe a little *ego* could help," Judy says.

"Oh come on, Judy! What can my ego do for me?"

"Ask not what your ego can do for you, ask what you can do for your ego."*

After giving it some thought I think I know just what could do the trick, so a few days later I decide all by myself to do something for myself and my ego. Without my parents' permission I go downtown and with the money I've saved babysitting I buy myself my very first

---

jolt, to jump suddenly
ego, here: how well a person thinks of himself
* This sentence refers to the famous words John F. Kennedy once said: "Ask not what your country can do for you, ask what you can do for your country."

pair of high-heels! They're red. They're shiny. They're just perfect. And I am going to wear them to the Thanksgiving Day dance no matter what! Of course I will have to keep them a secret from my parents. My original idea is to stuff them in the closet and then put them on when I'm out of the house. But as luck would have it, my mother sees me returning from my shopping trip. There was never any way I could hide anything from her.

"What'd you buy?" she asks, her x-ray eyes *piercing* through my shopping bag. I have no choice but to show her my shoes.

"Oh, how could you spend your money on something useless like that?" she cries out impatiently, looking deep into the depths of my soul.

Who knows what it is she sees all the way down there, but whatever it is, it makes her say with a sigh, "Okay, put them on and walk. Show Mommy how you walk."

I put on my new heels and somewhat *wobbly* I walk up and down the living-room floor.

"Jerry, Jerry," my mother suddenly cries out. "Come, hurry!"

My father rushes out of the bathroom. "What's the matter?" he cries out. "Did a train crash through the bedroom window or something?"

"Walk for Daddy," my mother commands. "Walk."

Once again I model my shoes.

"Do you see, Jerry," my mother's excited voice cries out. "Do you see?"

---

pierce, here: to make a hole
wobbly, unsteady

"What am I, blind?" And then turning to me he shouts, "I'll be a *son of a gun*. You're walking straight. My daughter's walking straight! Just like a little lady. I knew you could if you just tried."

"Sweetheart!" yells my mother.

"Princess!" cries out my father.

"My ears!" screams Joycey.

Peppy barks hysterically, Davey laughs, and I see my face light up and turn into sunshine - pure, one hundred percent sunshine.

---

son of a gun, here: a slang expression of disbelief

9. An Update

And that's the story of what happened one fine day when I was thirteen, more or less how I learned to walk straight. Now, some of you may try to find a moral to the story. If you do find one you're welcome to keep it, but don't ask me to take responsibility for its *validity*. My only intention was to tell you a simple tale about what it felt like to be a teenager in New York over twenty-five years ago. Nothing more and nothing less. So *go easy on* the morals if you can help it, okay?

But since I'm the type of person who likes neat and tidy endings I will give you a quick update on the story.

After I bought the high-heels, my pigeon-toes did not immediately disappear. Walking straight took concentration. I had to put one foot straight in front of the other. But since I was a young lady who had learned to live with disappointment by believing in herself and her ego, walking straight and concentrating became easier. In any case, I walked nicely enough to get rid of those awful orthopedic shoes.

My cheerleading career was a success. I improved my footwork and remained – as Mrs. Woo-Chang expressed it – enthusiastic and energetic. However, when I entered high school a few years later I decided to join the writers' club instead.

My parents no longer live in New York. A few years ago they moved to the West, to the desert in Nevada, where the closest elevated subway is at least 400 miles

---

validity, truthfulness
go easy on, (slang) be careful with

away. And they are now the proud owners of two color televisions.

My brother Davey did learn to be a forward and outgoing man. He now lives in San Francisco with his wife, his baby daughter and his shy and withdrawn son who he sends on weekend camping trips whenever he can.

My sister Joycey found love and the joys of motherhood in southern California. Three days a week she teaches math at the local high school.

My best friend Judy O'Reilly never existed. Sorry. She's just a character I made up, a *figment* of my imagination – a *composite* of all the girlfriends I ever had.

Fat-Face-Frankie Moronelli came back into my life. The following summer he was sent to a camp for overweight youngsters. He returned 40 pounds lighter and at least a thousand times nicer. He apologized and asked me out to the Beatles concert in Forest Hills Stadium. After that we dated for a while, but not long enough to ever try "it."

I did forget Mark, but never the way he touched me in the park that autumn afternoon.

And remember the fellow I had a date with recently? The one I almost bought a new slinky, silky black dress for that didn't fit? Well, it's not going to work out with him. But don't worry, it's okay. And do you know why? Because he wears white boxer shorts. Really! With pictures of farm animals on them! And no matter how

---

figment, something that doesn't really exist
composite the entire thing; the whole that is made up of different parts

much I try, I can't quite imagine spending a *chunk* of my life with someone who wears underwear with chickens and cows printed on them.

And my friend, the computer expert who considers me the second-most intelligent woman he has ever met and thinks my IQ is 148? Well, he calls me up this afternoon and tells me he happened to meet that politician who's the most intelligent woman he knows. But after talking to her, he tells me, he now believes that she's only the third-most intelligent. He says I get to stay in second place but he's leaving first place open for a while and if I want to I can try out for it when I find the time.

So I laugh and tell him that I don't have time for things like that. I tell him that nothing like that matters any more. I say I feel perfectly fine just where I am, that I don't have to be the best or the most of anything. And while I'm saying that, I'm thinking how much fun it is talking to this guy, how much I like him. And I wonder why I haven't ever realized it before. Suddenly the room begins to glow and I look out the window. It's a brilliant and crisp autumn afternoon – royal blue sky, puffy, white clouds, bright, stark sunlight. And I think, well, maybe I should go for it.

"Listen," I say to him. "Listen, would you like to come over this evening for dinner? I have this computer program with a virus and I thought you might like to investigate it."

And you know what? He's coming. Believe me, you never know what can happen one fine day ....

---

chunk, a big piece

ONE FINE DAY
OR
How I Learned
To walk Straight

President John F. Kennedy.
May 29, 1917 – November 22, 1963.

November 22, 1963 – President John F. Kennedy approximately one minute before he was shot in Dallas, Texas. His wife Jacqueline is seated next to him. In front of them are Governor John Connally of Texas and his wife.

November 24, 1963 – In a Dallas jail Lee Harvey Oswald (center), the accused assassin of President Kennedy, is attacked by nightclub owner Jack Ruby (right). A policeman looks on (left). Oswald died several hours later.

November 25, 1963 – The funeral of President Kennedy. Among the mourners are Kennedy's children Caroline and John F. Kennedy Jr. (John-John), the President's wife Jacqueline, and his brothers Attorney General Robert Kennedy and Senator Edward Kennedy.

A typical New York City 8th grade class during the school year 1963 – 1964. The future author of *ONE FINE DAY, or How I Learned to Walk Straight* is among the smiling faces. She is the one wearing the dirty white sneakers 4th from right, bottom row.

Holly-Jane Rahlens as The Narrator in the German television production of *One Fine Day*.

Questions

1

1. What is an IQ?
2. Why does the narrator go up to Miss Cohen's desk?
3. What was the narrator's "specialty" when she was thirteen years old?
4. What does the narrator buy instead of a fancy dress?
5. How does the narrator describe herself today?

* * *

6. Did you ever take an intelligence test? If so, what was it like?
7. Do you know what your IQ is?
8. When was the last time you lied, and what was the lie?
9. What do you think is more interesting: fact or fiction?
10. Describe yourself ten years ago.

2

1. Where and when does the story take place?
2. What is the weather like when the story begins?

3. What does Judy O'Reilly wear to make her teeth straight?
4. What does the narrator wear to make her feet straight?
5. What is pigeon-toed?
6. With whom is the narrator in love?
7. What does the narrator like to read when she stretches herself out on the bed?

* * *

8. Describe the street and town where you live.
9. Nobody is perfect. Is there something about yourself, you wish was different?
10. Do you think the narrator is really in love with Mark Lieberman?

3

1. Who is in the park?
2. What are the boys doing in the park?
3. What happens during the break?
4. What does Fat-Face-Frankie Moronelli call the narrator, and what does she call him?

* * *

5. Do you think the narrator really has a chance to win Mark's heart?

6. Have you ever played basketball? If so, explain the rules.
7. Were you ever in seventh heaven? What was it like?
8. Why do you think Mark doesn't defend the narrator against Fat-Face-Frankie?
9. Did you ever have to defend yourself? Describe what happened.
10. What is "it" and why do we have such a hard time talking about it?

4

1. Where do Judy and the narrator hide away from Fat-Face-Frankie Moronelli?
2. What did the narrator steal from her mother?
3. What awful news does Judy tell the narrator?
4. Who is Glenda Lapidus?
5. What is a cheerleader?

* * *

6. Do you have a secret hiding place? Can you describe it, or is it still too secret to tell?
7. What kind of music do you like to listen to with your friends?
8. Have you ever given or received an ID bracelet, or something like it?

9. Have you ever seen cheerleaders? What was your impression?
10. Do you think the narrator should fight for Mark?

5

1. Who are Davey and Joycey? Describe them.
2. What is the narrator's mother doing when we first see her?
3. How do the narrator's parents earn their living?
4. What does the narrator's mother do to her hair?
5. Why can't the narrator wear high-heels?

* * *

6. Describe the members of your family.
7. Do you help your brother or sister with his or her homework, or do they help you?
8. Do your parents yell at you? Why?
9. Why do you think the narrator's father is in such a bad mood?
10. Why do you think the narrator starts to cry?

6

1. What does Mrs. Woo-Chang tell the girls in gym class?

2. Why does the narrator want to become a cheerleader?
3. Where does the narrator practice the cheers?
4. Who is on the jury?
5. Mrs. Woo-Chang says the narrator has two special qualities. What are they?
6. What does the narrator have to do before the first game of the season?

* * *

7. What kind of games do you play during gym class?
8. Did you ever have to try out for something? If so, what was it like?
9. Do you think cheerleading is a sensible activity?
10. Do you have a goal in life too?

7

1. Where will Mark and the narrator go on their first date?
2. Name the different classes the narrator has to go to on this day.
3. Who is crying over the school's loudspeaker?
4. Why is the basketball game canceled?

5. Why does Mark go home with Glenda and not with the narrator?

* * *

6. What did you do on your very first date?
7. Do you sometimes find school a torture too? Why?
8. What else do you know about John F. Kennedy and the Kennedy family?
9. The narrator is unhappy that the basketball game is canceled, but not that the president has been assassinated. Do you understand her, or do you think she is wrong to be like that?
10. Can you remember a day you will never forget? Describe what happened.

8

1. Where does the narrator spend her time after the death of Kennedy?
2. Who is Lee Harvey Oswald and what happens to him?
3. Who is Jack Ruby and what does he do?
4. What does the narrator buy downtown?
5. What happens when the narrator puts on her new high-heels?

* * *

6. A whole nation saw Lee Harvey Oswald being shot on live television. Do you think things like that should be shown on TV?
7. Were you ever shocked by something you saw on television?
8. The narrator buys herself a pair of high-heels. Is there something special you would love to buy for yourself?
9. Do you think we have to show our parents everything we buy?
10. Why do you think the narrator can suddenly walk straight?

9

1. What club did the narrator join when she entered high school?
2. What are the members of her family doing now?
3. Which person in the story never really existed?
4. What happened to Fat-Face-Frankie Moronelli?
5. Who does the narrator have a dinner date with in the evening?

* * *

6. The narrator says her story doesn't have a moral, but maybe it does. If so, what do you think it could be?

7. How do you feel about Judy O'Reilly not being real?
8. Why do you think the narrator told us this story in the first place?
9. Let your imagination run wild. Describe what you think the narrator is like today. Where does she live? What does she do to earn a living? Do you like her? etc.
10. What do you think could happen to you one fine day?